D1084846

HAPPINESS IS A STOCK THAT LETS YOU SLEEP AT NIGHT

HAPPINESS IS A STOCK THAT LETS YOU SLEEP AT NIGHT

Ira U. Cobleigh

A BERNARD GEIS ASSOCIATES BOOK
PUBLISHED BY DONALD I. FINE, INC.
NEW YORK

Library of Congress Cataloging-in-Publication Data

Cobleigh, Ira U.
  Happiness is a stock that lets you sleep at night.

    1. Stocks. 2. Investments. I. Title.
HG6041.C59   1988   332.63'22   88-45804
ISBN 1-55611-119-3

Design: Stanley S. Drate/Folio Graphics Co. Inc.

Manufactured in the United States of America

10 9 8 7 6 5 4 3 2 1

CONTENTS

A WORD TO THE MONEY-WISE

The crash of October 1987 notably changed the views of investors, Wall Street brokers and portfolio managers. Previously fashionable investments in computer, growth, and technology stocks, as well as "sector" funds and highly leveraged speculations involving margin accounts, options and indexes proved disastrous. There is now a visible swing back to quality stocks with solid earnings and dependable dividends. I welcome this and offer in this book season and I believe sound counsel to the 47 million investors in common stocks in the United States.

The election of George Bush as President makes the publication of this book especially timely. The new administration is facing a host of economic challenges, ranging from the budget and trade deficits to the risk of inflation and the possibility of subsequent recession. The thirty strong and well-managed companies recommended in this book have been selected, to a large extent, on the basis of their ability to weather in good health the transitional period immediately ahead. There will be opportunities as well as risks in the coming years, and these companies are particularly well positioned to take advantage of the many opportunities the United States and global economies offer for the future.

The reader will note that each of these companies stands on its own feet. There is not a mutual fund in the entire group. The movement away from stock mutual funds is a noteworthy trend. Their presumed virtues of continuous professional portfolio management and the protection of broad diversification did not prevent or cushion their precipitous fall in value. Indeed, over 60% of stock mutual funds failed to outperform the Dow Jones Industrial Average both in the first six months of 1987 and in the disastrous week of October 19. "Buy and Hold" investors holding such blue chip stocks as Exxon, General Electric, NYNEX, Consolidated Edison and Heinz reported higher retentions of portfolio values than mutuals, or random lists of lower grade, more or less speculative securities.

This 1987 crisis proves the wisdom of an investment credo held by millions of "old timers": buy good stocks with steady or rising earnings and dividend expectations, and don't try to trade them in and out on short-term swings. Remember, the average recession lasts only eighteen months. It is better to wait it out than to sell, pay capital gain taxes, and then perhaps lose out on a stock dividend or split. The message of this book is to upgrade your stocks and to trade less. Forget about technical charts, options and indexes. Keep your dollars in money market funds for short term or market reentry and confine yourself over the long term to the thirty premier stocks we have researched. I call them "Fortress Stocks" and am convinced that they will, over time, outperform the majority of the mutual funds. They will provide dependable growth and gain in income and principal. And, most importantly, they will provide that priceless ingredient—the kind of investment security that lets you sleep serenely the whole night through.

THE NEW MARKET CLIMATE

The inspiration for this book came from the market earthquake on October 19, 1987, the most massive sell-off in the history of finance. Stocks on the New York Stock Exchange declined by 508 points (22.6%) on the Dow Jones Industrial Average, and the volume was a fantastic 604 million shares—more than three times the usual volume of shares traded on a single day. Immediately, comparisons were drawn with the 1929 crash. Some notes on that earlier event therefore seem appropriate.

The 1929 Crash
■ ■ ■

The 1929 model was mainly a credit crisis. There were, in those days, only 1.5 million stock owners (compared to 47 million investors today), and no mutual funds. The trouble started by making stock purchase too easy! By putting down $1,000 with your broker you could purchase $10,000 in market value of a stock—a thin 10% margin, as opposed to 50% required nowadays. When the market soared, as it did in 1928 and 1929, it was easy to make a killing, and these "paper profits" funded additional purchases. The speculative darlings of that era were Radio Corporation, Technicolor, Allied Chemical and Dye, Electric Bond and Share, General Motors and North American Company. Pyramided utility holding companies were the equivalent of leveraged buy-outs today.

The market was provincial then, with few foreign investors in American stocks. The dollar was sound and convertible into gold at $20.67 an ounce. Only 16.3 million shares traded on a single day in October 1929. (Today, the daily average is close to 200 million shares traded.) The Dow fell from a high of 381.17 in 1929 to a low of 41.22 in 1932—an 85% plunge.

CALL MONEY

The big trouble was the bloated extension of credit—"call loans" (secured by stock collateral), which supplied as much as 80% of the funds advanced by brokers to their margin customers. This lending of call money was amazingly profitable. Banks could borrow from the Federal Reserve Bank ("the Fed") at 4% and lend the funds out to brokerage houses at rates of 12%

to 15%, and sometimes higher. Banks prospered and their shares zoomed. The real culprit in all this frantic speculation was not brokers pushing up stocks, or tips planted by market manipulators, but easy money from the Fed. Available money and too-thin margins overwhelmed the "suckers" and accelerated the depression.

PANIC SELLING

When the market plunged in October 1929, speculators scrambled to answer margin calls: to put up more cash to protect fading security values. As the market fell further, more margin calls went out. Tens of thousands of speculators were wiped out and had to sell or mortgage their homes. And so the depression steadily deepened.

Later, commodity prices fell, impoverishing farmers and businesses. Railroads went into bankruptcy and, at the bottom, unemployment reached 25%. Home ownership in those times was perilous if there was a mortgage. First mortgages on homes generally commanded 6% interest. Mortgages ran for three to five years with no amortization. When, for instance, a $5,000 mortgage came due, the whole $5,000 became payable. The owner might get the bank to extend or renew the mortgage for another term. But if he couldn't renew, he had to raise the $5,000 or the house was foreclosed. From 1929 to 1932, with thousands wiped out by market losses, there was a national epidemic of home foreclosures. (An ironic note: In my community, a house that was foreclosed for $6,000 in 1932 recently sold for $200,000.)

1987 Was Different
■ ■ ■

The October 1987 market crash also spawned a spate of margin calls, although investors on 50% margins were far less pressed than the 1929 crop of speculators.

There was, in 1987, no broad financial panic, with banks closing, mortgages foreclosed, and the like. We now have strong platforms bolstering the economy, platforms that were nonexistent in 1929: bank deposit insurance up to $100,000, Social Security income for senior citizens, unemployment insurance, student loans and other resources. Moreover, 68 million of us own our own homes, many with substantial equity in them. There is nothing like the erosion of assets and income that occurred in 1929.

The Global Market
■ ■ ■

On the negative side, one significant problem today is that the stock market is no longer provincial but worldwide, with billions invested by wealthy Arabs,

Asians, Japanese, British and Germans. Thus when a selling stampede occurs, it is not just Americans unloading. In October 1987, when Wall Street plunged, so did the markets in London, Tokyo and Hong Kong. Selling climaxes in 1987 were accelerated by computerized trading programs, portfolio insurance, index futures and stock options. They were also speeded by the need of mutual funds to sell stock in heavy volume to redeem the fund shares of their customers who wanted out. There was considerable fund liquidation on October 19, but the index transactions were probably even more responsible for the high volatility of the market. To illustrate that volatility, note that J. P. Morgan, America's most elite bank stock, was driven from 41⅝ to 27¾ on October 19, rebounded to 40 a couple of days later, only to fall back again and trade in the high 30s.

In view of the foregoing observations, what are the prospects for the economy in the next few years? It definitely won't be a reprise of 1929. Because of the renewed efficiency of American companies, and major restructuring in recent years, profits should be well sustained. Markets will be supported by the programs of more than three hundred companies who plan repurchase of their own shares.

The lower dollar has made American companies more competitive abroad. If only we can achieve significant reduction in the national trade deficits, our economy may reclaim much of its earlier vigor. Labor costs have not accelerated to any great extent, and many corporations are reporting record earnings. The bottom line: no depression!

The October 1987 crash was not the end of the world. It may well be that, with a half-trillion-dollar reduction in net worth, Americans will lessen their purchases of Mercedes, condominiums, forty-foot cruisers and beach cottages. But America will continue its forward motion.

The specific objective here is to improve your selection of stocks and the making of portfolio decisions. Avoid index options, margin accounts and stock options (which lose almost 70% of the time). Also avoid virtually all of the over two hundred investment products a customer's broker can now offer you. Avoid sector trusts, unit trusts, speculative new issues and frantic trading by technical charts. Place less reliance on stock mutual funds, many of which have displayed mediocre management. Instead, prepare to consider and welcome the thirty extensively researched Fortress Stocks, designed to reduce your risk and maximize your net worth. The purchase and retention of these high-quality stocks over several years will prove greatly rewarding.

The crashes of 1929 and 1987 have lessons for all of us. Remember, in the market nothing recedes like excess! With the Dow Jones Industrial Average in the 2500–2600 range just prior to the 1987 crash on October 19, stocks were too high!

WHY JUST THIRTY FORTRESS STOCKS?

Why just thirty stocks? Because this is the number found sufficient for diversification. The Dow Jones Industrial Average contains just thirty stocks. The Lipper Over the Counter list contains thirty stocks. The Blue Chip Value Fund invests in just twenty-five issues selected from three hundred of the largest dividend-paying companies in the United States. The fund, which was formed in 1987 by a respected syndicate of Wall Street investment firms, operates on the same investment philosophy that prompted our selection of thirty Fortress Stocks. My view is that unless your portfolio exceeds $10 million there is no need for more than thirty top-drawer equities. Diversification is usually described as "not putting all your eggs in one basket." In textbooks on investment, diversification is the spreading of security holdings in such a way that one or two losing issues may not imperil the whole list. The concept makes a lot of sense, but has been greatly overdone. How many different issues do you really need in your portfolio for a consistently winning performance?

If you examine the prospectus of a big mutual fund with a portfolio of a billion dollars or more, you'll note it lists a holding of hundreds of different stocks and bond issues.

The Magellan Fund, one of the largest, has over sixteen hundred issues. For these big institutional investors, such a spread of risks is inevitable because so many dollars have to be kept at work. But the clustering of holdings in very large blocks might impair their marketability when the time comes for selling. And if thousands of mutual fund holders converge on a mutual fund office at once, wishing to redeem their shares, the fund may have to dump stocks on the market under adverse conditions.

October 19, 1987, was the moment of truth for mutual funds. They were tested as never before. Investors called in droves to liquidate their shares. (Fidelity Funds had over two hundred thousand phone calls October 19, 1987.) Many investors chose not to sell out, but to swiftly convert their stock funds into money market funds to defend against further market losses.

Dreyfus, with some $40 billion in its funds, found that for every holder who insisted on redemption there were ten others who instead switched to money market funds or short-term government portfolios.

Hardest hit were the smaller independent funds that offered no alternate vehicle to switch into. So desperate was the wave of liquidation that many smaller mutuals suffered heavy customer losses. For many investors this was the first market crisis they had ever encountered.

It is important to note that on October 19 the majority of funds performed worse than the Dow or Standard & Poor's indexes. Several respected funds lost 40% or more in portfolio value, particularly those invested in secondary, technology or less active over-the-counter issues.

In view of the sell-off of bond funds earlier in 1987 and the general performance of stock funds later that year, individuals will be better off in the long run with a portfolio of our thirty Fortress Stocks. I am confident that our thirty Fortress Stocks will regularly outperform most mutual funds.

In reviewing the portfolios of dozens of successful investors (having spent years as a financial editor), I have noted many individuals who have done very well by holding only about twenty or thirty stocks carefully selected among dominant companies in different industries. Effective diversification seems to be a matter more of quality than quantity.

Berkshire Hathaway, a brilliantly managed holding company, has confined itself to only a dozen or so companies. The Rockefellers did well by concentrating on their Standard Oil shares. The Watson family bathed in wealth simply by holding onto their IBM.

The Dow Jones Industrial Average, made up of

only thirty stocks, has proved to be just as useful an indicator for total market performance as the Standard & Poor's Index of five hundred.

Our conclusion is that diversification has been overrated, and that when companies and industries selected are not related to one another, the results are excellent—because risks are efficiently spread.

The Renowned Dow Jones Industrial Average
■ ■ ■

A book entitled *Happiness Is a Stock that Lets You Sleep at Night* should certainly contain a description of the Dow Jones Industrial Average, a historic recorder of the combined performance of many of the finest stocks in the world. Indeed, our own tailored list of thirty Fortress Stocks includes several of the Dow issues.

Whenever you read a news account about Wall Street, comment in the financial press, or listen to a market summary on radio or television, you are certain to hear about the Dow Jones Industrial Average (DJIA). It is the universally respected index of stock prices and market motion. The DJIA is as well-known in London, Hong Kong and Tokyo as in New York. It made world headlines and history when it fell 508 points on Black Monday, October 19, 1987.

How did this index originate and who decides what

stocks are included? This first stock index was the creation of Charles Dow, the first editor of the *Wall Street Journal* and one of the founders of Dow Jones & Company.

As the stock market expanded in tandem with the economic growth of the United States, Mr. Dow thought that a performance index was needed to document daily market action and perhaps to serve as a useful barometer to indicate the possible future direction of stock prices. Such an index, he thought, might provide guidance to investors for the better timing of their buy and sell decisions.

Dow started out by selecting eleven actively traded stocks—nine railroads and only two industrials. He calculated the first "Dow Average" by adding the closing prices of these shares and dividing the total by eleven. The first Dow Jones Average, thus calculated, was published July 3, 1894.

As the number of issues listed on the New York Stock Exchange and the volume of trading rose, changes became necessary. More stocks were added to make the list more diversified and representative. The number of stocks was expanded to twelve in 1896, to twenty in 1916, and finally to thirty, the present number, in 1928.

Revisions in the stocks comprising the DJIA need to be made from time to time as companies merge, go bankrupt or become no longer relevant, or as companies in newer industries gain stature. These changes in the list are made independently by the editors of the

Wall Street Journal. There is no consultation with the Securities and Exchange Commission, The New York Stock Exchange (all DJIA companies are listed on NYSE) or individual company managements. The stocks now on the list were chosen from major industrial companies covering a cross-section of the American economy and account for a third of the assets of industrial America.

The Current List of DJIA

The current Dow Jones list of thirty industrial stocks follows:

Alcoa	Exxon*†
Allied Signal*	General Electric*
American Express†	General Motors*
AT&T†	Goodyear
Bethlehem Steel*	IBM
Boeing	International Paper
Chevron	McDonald's†
Coca-Cola†	Merck†
Du Pont	Minnesota M&M†
Eastman Kodak	Navistar*

*These companies were on the list of the original thirty on October 1, 1928.

†These companies are on our own selected list of thirty Fortress Stocks.

(Allied Signal was originally known as Allied Chemical; Exxon as Standard Oil, N.J.; Navistar as International Harvester; Primerica as American Can Co.; USX as US Steel.)

Philip Morris   Union Carbide*
Primerica*   United Technologies
Proctor & Gamble†   USX*
Sears Roebuck*   Westinghouse*
Texaco   Woolworth*

Only twelve of the above companies were on the original list of thirty on October 1, 1928. Stocks active and popular at that time, such as Victor Talking Machine, Nash Motors, Postum and Mack Trucks, have since been displaced.

In all, there have been thirty-two substitutions in the DJIA since 1928, the most recent being the replacement in 1987 of Owen Illinois Glass and Inco by Coca-Cola and Boeing. Coca-Cola had been added (1932) to replace Hudson Motor, but was in turn replaced (1935) by National Steel. IBM replaced National Cash Register in 1932 but was dumped in favor of AT&T in 1939. IBM returned to the list in 1979 when it displaced Chrysler.

The most newsworthy feature of the DJIA is the daily closing price. This is noted and reported each day around the world. Sharp day-to-day variations in this closing quote influence the investment decisions of millions of individual and institutional investors globally.

The range of these closing prices has been dramatic. As was noted earlier, the all-time low was 41.22 in 1932 and the historic high was 2722.42 on August 12, 1987. The 1929 high was 381.17. This was not topped until 1954, when a high of 404.39 was recorded. The Dow never crossed 1000 until 1972 and never went beyond 2000 until 1987. The largest loss ever in a single day was 508 points on October 19, 1987, when the Dow fell by 22.6% and total market value of securities was melted down by over half a trillion dollars!

T·H·R·E·E

SCREENING THE FORTRESS SELECTIONS

Lhe group of thirty Fortress Stocks was screened down from over 125 companies that appeared to have the proper qualifications. The criterion used for selection of each was "How well will this stock perform over a five-year period" in terms of (1) protection (or enhancement) of principal, (2) maintenance and probable increase in dividends, (3) competence and "drive" of management, (4) financial structure (low debt), (5) capacity to innovate and expand by introduction of new products or services or compatible acquisitions, and (6) perception and disposal of "tired" divisions that are not generating desired profit margins.

In designing the list, I also wanted to be sure the investment was not just a popular selection of a "name" company, used to dress up a portfolio. To illustrate, many may wonder why IBM, the computer virtuoso, was not included. The reason is that IBM has grown so big that its growth potential has virtually dried up. Competitors have invaded the computer markets, both for mainframes and personal computers, so that IBM is no longer dominant, and the technology developed among some of the younger companies in this industry has challenged the historic technological preeminence of IBM. IBM is a classic stock, but it has arrived at a comfortable plateau and lost much of its forward motion.

General Electric, too, is found in most blue-chip stock lists. It is a great company with a great record. But a third of its activity is in the defense industry, which may slow down with budget austerity in Washington. Moreover, the light bulb business is not as profitable as it was before; ditto appliance manufacturing. General Electric's acquisition of Kidder Peabody does not look like a work of genius, and RCA, another GE acquisition, has lost much of its luster. While GE will continue to be a leading stock, no great upsurge in profits in the next two years is perceived. Furthermore, the potential for their dividend to increase appears minimal. GE was therefore omitted.

Boeing, a solid company, might have been selected a few years ago. Now it seems too heavily involved in defense, a precarious position in a Washington budget cut. And Boeing has had a hard time bringing new model production into a maximized profit range.

Equally, General Dynamics, an industrial giant, does not qualify at the progressive level. Being among the largest defense contractors makes it vulnerable as well. For both Boeing and General Dynamics we think profit generation is a little too uneven to merit long-term passive ownership of their shares.

There were not only many major stocks that were passed over, but indeed whole industries as well, where the risks are too great and representative companies too volatile in their earning power. For instance, the advertising industry has proved profitable—yet leaders here have suffered critical losses of major accounts, personnel are notably migratory, and mergers have created confusion in the industry. We consider advertising just not stable enough to qualify as a Fortress holding.

Steel used to be a great industry, but leaders today are groping with restructurings, cutting down mill capacity and closing tired mills. And, of course, there has been fierce competition from foreign imports. Bethlehem and USX have shown excellent turnarounds, but their stocks are still well below blue-chip status.

In the same sense, machine toolers and machine manufacturers have not created favorable climates for conservative long-term investment.

Building and construction companies have slowed down. Originally, high mortgage interest was the chief deterrent, and now the fallout from the October 1987 Wall Street crash continues to create a negative effect in this industry.

Time was when Inco, Amax and Phelps Dodge

were metal blue chips, but now they are working hard to restore their former status as dependable moneymakers as copper, nickel and lead gain in price.

The Fortress Stocks list is based not on a popularity contest but on fundamental values and forward motion. While the Fortress list, as was noted, skipped over many industries and companies, the stocks we finally selected comprise an excellent cross-section of the American economy. The fortunes of these elite companies will wax and wane, but over the next several years this group will, in my view, outperform the Dow Jones Industrial Average—and a majority of stock mutual funds. These Fortress Stocks are selected for stature, quality, growth and income reliability. Along the way, many will increase their dividends, some will declare extras or split, and two or three might emerge as takeover candidates. Any portfolio with these entries is bound to be a long-term winner.

F·O·U·R

THE THIRTY FORTRESS STOCKS

We now present the list of thirty Fortress Stocks for long-term holding. Please note that the New York Stock Exchange symbol given under the name of each stock is not, in most cases, the listing used in newspaper quotations of the stock but the special symbol used by the Stock Exchange itself and by brokerage houses. Here they are, in alphabetical order.

29

American Express

American Telephone and Telegraph

Automatic Data Processing

Burlington Northern

Citicorp

Coca-Cola

Colgate-Palmolive

Consolidated Edison

Dow Chemical

Dun & Bradstreet

Exxon

Ford Motor Company

Kellogg

Marriott

Marsh & McLennan

May Department Stores

McDonald's

Merck

Minnesota Mining and Manufacturing

J.P. Morgan

Motorola

NYNEX

Potomac Electric Power

Proctor & Gamble

Royal Dutch Petroleum

Schlumberger

Seagram

Tri-Continental

Upjohn

Weyerhaeuser

The following chart shows what would have happened over the ten-year period, January 1, 1978, to December 31, 1987, if you had invested $1,000 in each of our thirty Fortress Stocks for a total investment of $30,000. Note that the investment grew to $137,461.37 for a gain of $107,461.37. The percentage of increase was 358%. During the same ten-year period the percentage of increase, including dividends, for the thirty stocks that comprise the Dow Jones Industrial Average was 208%.

RESULTS OF AN INVESTMENT OF $1,000 IN EACH OF THIRTY "FORTRESS STOCKS" HELD FOR TEN YEARS [1/1/78 to 12/31/87]—WITHOUT REINVESTMENT OR COMPOUND INTEREST

Company	Price Per Share 1/1/78*	Price Per Share 12/31/87	Ten Year Total Cash Dividends	Market Value Plus Dividends 12/31/87**
American Express	$ 8.94	$22 7/8	$ 645.94	$ 3,195.94
American Telephone & Telegraph†	7.70	27 1/8	593.60	4,115.50
Automatic Data Processing	7.14	44 7/8	354.20	6,636.00
Burlington Northern	10.21	62 3/4	962.64	7,102.10
Citicorp	11.68	18 3/4	816.04	2,419.91
Coca-Cola	12.12	38 1/8	707.60	3,851.77
Colgate-Palmolive	21.25	39	568.70	2,401.70
Consolidated Edison	12.69	41 3/4	1,476.08	4,732.58
Dow Chemical	26.00	90 1/4	669.22	4,140.23
Dun & Bradstreet	7.68	54 3/4	1,096.26	8,218.14
Exxon	11.84	38 1/4	1,262.38	4,492.21
Ford Motor Company	20.48	75 1/4	602.00	4,289.25
Kellogg	12.18	52 3/8	677.32	4,971.66
Marriott	2.28	30	327.99	13,377.98
Marsh & McLennan	15.27	49 1/2	759.10	3,998.36
May Department Stores	8.91	29 1/8	788.34	4,053.85
McDonald's	14.88	44	252.66	3,207.70
Merck	26.80	158 1/2	632.24	6,544.29
Minnesota Mining & Manuf.	23.37	69 3/4	658.82	3,642.72

*Adjusted for stock dividends and splits
**Original investment 1/1/78: $1,000
†The returns on American Telephone & Telegraph would have been over $2,000 higher if the seven operating company stocks spun off in 1984 had been included.

32

Company	Price Per Share 1/1/78*	Price Per Share 12/31/87	Ten Year Total Cash Dividends	Market Value Plus Dividends 12/31/87**
J.P. Morgan	$ 10.75	$ 36 1/4	$ 838.12	$ 4,173.00
Motorola	12.00	44 5/8	447.86	4,169.16
NYNEX††	30.00	64 1/4	1,074.80	3,130.80
Potomac Electric Power	7.75	21 7/8	1,169.54	3,968.67
Proctor & Gamble	42.87	84 1/2	436.50	2,307.33
Royal Dutch Petroleum	13.36	111 7/8	584.73	4,778.71
Schlumberger	21.13	28 7/8	438.12	1,804.71
Seagram	7.37	54 1/8	839.64	8,176.68
Tri-Continental	7.14	20 5/8	833.00	3,719.80
Upjohn	8.81	30	426.72	3,786.72
Weyerhaeuser	27.50	39 1/4	562.40	2,053.90

Total Market Value Plus Dividends 12/31/87 .... $137,461.37
Total Investment 1/1/78: $1,000 × 30 stocks 30,000.00
Total Investment Gain Over 10 Years $107,461.37
Total Percentage of Increase Over 10 Years 358%

RESULTS OF THE DJIA OVER TEN YEARS (1/1/78 to 12/31/87)—
WITHOUT REINVESTMENT OR COMPOUND INTEREST

Dow Jones Industrial Average (30 stocks) 12/31/87 .... 1,938.83
Total DJIA Dividends Over 10 Years 581.45
Total DJIA Market Value Plus Dividends 12/31/87 .... 2,520.45
Dow Jones Industrial Average 1/1/78 .... 817.74
Total DJIA Gain Over 10 Years 1,702.54
Total Percentage of Increase in DJIA Over 10 Years 208%

*Adjusted for stock dividends and splits.
**Original investment 1/1/78: $1,000.
††NYNEX, a spin-off from AT&T, started trading 11/1/83. That is the date used for an investment of $1,000. The market-value-and-dividends figure is thus for four years, instead of ten years as with the other stocks.

33

AMERICAN EXPRESS

■ ■ ■

NYSE Symbol: AXP

American Express is a massive combination of travel-related and financial services. It has proven its corporate capability by paying continuous cash dividends for 117 years in a row.

American Express started out transporting packaged goods on railroad lines—"travel related" from the outset. From that beginning, the company has exploded in size, merged, acquired and branched out so that today it is a global company with over $100 billion in assets.

Best known of its operations is American Express Travelers Cheques and Credit Cards. American Express has over 24 million cards in force, and some 2 million service establishments accept the card. Travel services include vacation and leisure services and business-travel activities. The area of most rapid growth is in travel services.

Next in importance is their Shearson Lehman division (60% owned), a leading investment banking and brokerage firm with 27,000 employees. In December 1987, Shearson Lehman acquired E.F. Hutton, a large retail brokerage firm with eighteen thousand employees. The combination creates the second largest firm in Wall Street, just after Merrill Lynch. Shearson Lehman had some setbacks in 1987 (including Black Monday) and will require some time to assimilate Hutton. But the business has been very profitable in the long run (over $300 million in profits in 1986). American Express sold 16 million shares of Shearson to the public in May 1987 for $574 million. Shearson slowed down in 1987, as one might expect, but with the Hutton retail facilities added and with efficient blending of resources and cost controls, this brokerage and investment banking sector is positioned to expand profitably.

Another American Express enterprise, IDS Financial Services, is a major mutual fund distributor and offers an assortment of financial and insurance services to institutions, businesses and individuals. IDS is in the mainstream of the new financial profession—financial planners serving individuals. Its staff of financial planners numbers over six thousand. It delivers around $100 million in profits annually.

There is also American Express Bank, Ltd., added in 1983, providing diversified banking services through ninety-nine offices in forty-three nations. Recent annual profits were $175 million.

The company, because of its stature, revenues and potentially expanding markets, is a long-term dependable earner, and its shares add diversity and quality to mature portfolios. Except for 1983 and 1987, net profits have expanded in each of the past eleven years.

American Express stock is indeed a Fortress Stock.

AMERICAN TELEPHONE AND TELEGRAPH COMPANY

■ ■ ■

NYSE Symbol: T

This is the holding company that remained after "Ma Bell" was broken up in 1984 into AT&T and the seven regional operating telephone companies. AT&T retained about $34 billion out of the original combined $150 billion in assets.

The principal business of AT&T continues to be the operation of what was the Long Lines division—national and international telephone communications. If you make an interstate long distance call it will probably be AT&T that handles it, although since deregulation significant competition has arisen from MCI and Sprint. The Long Lines division accounts for a bit more than half of company revenues.

The Network Systems division makes and services telephone products and equipment (either rented or owned) used by the seven operating companies. Computers, silicon chips and other electronic products are also manufactured in conjunction with a Technology Systems division.

The International Marketing division makes and markets telecommunication products in all foreign markets, often in joint ventures with foreign companies. There is a Federal Systems division that handles business with the government, supplying systems and service as well as extensive equipment for the Department of Defense.

Bell Laboratories, a creation of the original Ma Bell, is the research center for AT&T operations and for the seven regional operating companies.

The newest division, AT&T Credit Corporation, was formed just after the 1984 breakup and provides long-term credit to corporate customers. This sector has grown rapidly and has acquired assets of over $1.4 billion.

Expanding its penetration into the computer market, some years ago AT&T acquired Olivetti, an Italian maker of computers, business machines, and telephone equipment.

This capsule account is intended to outline the breadth and diversity of AT&T operations and to present the company as far more than a mere long distance telephone company. It is a manufacturer, research center and electronics company competing in several sectors with IBM.

It has taken some time for AT&T to coordinate its activities. In 1985, computer operations were losing about $1 billion a year, and restructuring of operations and layoff of thousands of personnel accounted for erratic profitability. Now, however, management has been tightened, costs controlled, and there is a pronounced up-curve in the profit trend. For example, earnings per share were depressed to 21 cents in 1986 but rose ninefold a year later to $1.85. Earnings per share should be much higher in the next several years. AT&T is beginning to fulfill its promise and hit its stride as essentially a technology company.

AT&T is an honored name among investors, with an unbroken record of cash dividends since 1881. Today AT&T is the most widely held U.S. common stock. Its billion shares are owned by about 3 million holders. The dividend is secure and should be increased in coming years. AT&T is surely a basic Fortress Stock.

AUTOMATIC DATA PROCESSING, INC.

■ ■ ■

NYSE Symbol: AUD

Automatic Data Processing, Inc. has been selected as the Fortress representative of the computer industry. It is the largest independent computer service firm in the U.S. and has had an outstanding growth rate of over 10% annually for twenty-five years. Its revenues have soared from $299 million in 1978 to over $1.5 million.

Automatic Data Processing has taken a commanding position in its field and now has about 180,000 customers. Its clients cover a wide range of operations: brokerage, banking, automobile dealers, government divisions, business corporations and institutional clients. Payroll processing and brokerage operations represent the fastest growing sectors.

For automobile dealers, the company may provide inventory controls, collision and claim estimates, accounts payable and receivable, general invoicing and payroll accounting. For brokerage firms, Automatic Data Processing may handle trading, confirmations, stocks and customer records and statements and automatic quotation services. In fact, brokerage is the leading sector of operations. Latest developments are contracts with Shearson Lehman and Merrill Lynch for specially designed quotation systems. For banking operations there are electronic fund transfers, batch processing, and automatic teller accounting and control services.

All these services may seem routine, but they are essential to low-cost reporting, recording and payroll systems, and are being improved by research and innovations instituted by Automatic Data Processing management. Operations are regularly analyzed and unprofitable areas improved or closed down.

The company has done a good job not only in rapid expansion of revenues but in client retention. For thousands of companies, Automatic Data Processing services have become virtually indispensable.

Automatic Data has been a consistent moneymaker, annually increasing its earnings per share fourfold over the last nine years.

Automatic Data Processing is widely favored by institutions (which own over 70% of the 77 million shares outstanding) and is actively traded on the New

York Stock Exchange. Dividend payout is low (about 25% of net), but cash payments have been increased annually for more than a decade and share owners have been further rewarded by 100% stock dividends in 1981 and 1986. Increases in the price of the stock have more than offset the modest yield.

BURLINGTON NORTHERN, INC.

■ ■ ■

NYSE Symbol: BNI

Burlington Northern has been selected as a For-tress Stock because it is rich in property, durable in earnings and offers an excellent diversified blend of transportation and natural resource assets. It is also a rewarding dividend payer, continuous since 1940. There were 100% stock dividends in 1980 and 1984.

Burlington operates over 25,000 miles of railway lines serving twenty-five states and parts of Canada. Major freight revenues are derived from coal, forest products, grain and piggyback traffic.

Through a subsidiary, Meridian Oil Company, Burlington is an important oil and gas producer, controlling almost 5 million net acres sheltering proved reserves of more than 93 million barrels of crude and 3 trillion cubic feet of natural gas. Meridian also operates a 700-mile pipeline in Texas. Its extensive El Paso Natural Gas Company owns and operates a 21,700-mile pipeline system in the Southwest.

Plum Creek Timber Company, a subsidiary, produces a diversity of forest products from over 1.5 million acres of timber land. Burlington also owns property sheltering 14.5 billion tons of bituminous coal, which contributes substantial annual royalties.

In 1988 Burlington Northern created Burlington Resources as a separate company to include five of its non-railroad related businesses: Meridian Oil, El Paso Natural Gas, Plum Creek Timber, Meridian Minerals and Glacier Park Company. At the same time, 13% of the stock in Burlington Resources was publicly offered; the balance, 130 million shares, was distributed to Burlington Northern share owners.

In addition, the company operates and manages 1.3 million acres of farmland, has an urban real estate development division and owns six motor carrier companies with routes all across the country.

Burlington also owns 4.3 million additional acres, but this property has been restricted from use or development by the terms of non-callable bonds issued in 1890. There are $117 million of these bonds in public hands and Burlington has recently concluded an agreement to pay $35.5 million extra to these bond-holders in return for their agreement to release this acreage for active development. This opens up new horizons for profit for the company.

From the foregoing capsule account, one can get some idea of the magnitude of this company and the diversified sources of its earning power. Burlington certainly has the stamina required for a long-term investment holding.

Earnings are in an up-trend. This suggests a further boost in dividends, which were increased seven times in the last decade, including a recent 10% boost.

There are 74 million shares outstanding. The company has over 40,000 share owners. Burlington is, in our view, the best railway equity on the horizon.

CITICORP

■ ■ ■

NYSE Symbol: CCI

This global banking giant combines quality and yield with $200 billion in assets and is one of the largest banking companies in the world. It is a diversified financial service organization, deriving its expanding revenues from commercial and investment banking as well as from consumer banking. Citicorp has the best worldwide network and one of the broadest gauged and most profitable consumer banking franchises in the United States.

In the 1970s Citicorp came under criticism for the overly rapid buildup of its consumer sector. Expansion in this area, however, has now paid off, with recent return on equity of over 16%. Citicorp has a dominant slice of the New York consumer market and a presence in three of the four remaining top U.S. consumer markets: California, Illinois and Florida. It has done this by acquiring a series of heretofore poorly managed savings institutions. Citicorp also leads the nation in credit card issuance and the origination and service of mortgage loans.

In international banking and investment banking, Citicorp is the recognized leader in European commercial paper underwriting, foreign exchange trading and interest and currency swaps.

Since 1985, management has proved to be imaginative and aggressive in building deposits and improving cost controls.

Citicorp has been consistently identified with banking innovations. It first introduced personal loans in 1928, and in the 1970s it greatly expanded its consumer banking franchise when banks were generally moving in other directions. Citicorp, as indicated, has been one of the most aggressive advocates of credit cards.

The company has 159 million shares outstanding. It or its predecessors have paid continuous cash dividends since 1813.

Citicorp has been selected as a Fortress Stock because of its global stature, managerial competence in depth, rising earning power and balance sheet strength, and expanded capital base from recent stock financing.

THE COCA-COLA COMPANY

■ ■ ■

NYSE Symbol: KO

Coca-Cola has the best beverage franchise in the world and is the largest producer of soft drinks. No trademark is better known globally. Brand Coca-Cola and Diet Coke rank, respectively, numbers one and three in U.S. unit sales volume. Additional popular soft-drink sellers include Tab, Sprite, Fresca, Cherry Coke and Minute Maid soda.

Other well-known Coca-Cola products are Minute Maid orange juice and fruit juices marketed under the Hi-C and Bacardi labels. A factor in the successful marketing of its beverages is the company's 49% ownership of Coca-Cola Enterprises, its largest bottler.

Coca-Cola makes soft-drink syrups and concentrates and markets them to independent and company-owned bottlers and beverage wholesalers.

A few years ago, Coca-Cola acquired Columbia Pictures, which brought the company into the entertainment industry in a major way. This division was substantially augmented in 1986 when Coca-Cola purchased (for $250 million) Merv Griffin Enterprises, owner and producer of successful TV game shows, including "Wheel of Fortune," the most successful of all current game shows.

In October 1987, Coca-Cola exchanged these entertainment assets for 74 million shares of Tri-Star Pictures. It later distributed a portion of these shares to Coca-Cola share-owners but retained about 49% of Tri-Star. More recently, Tri-Star changed its name to Columbia Pictures Entertainment, whose shares are actively traded on the New York Stock Exchange, and is now expected to deliver about 20% of the total corporate profits of Coca-Cola.

Coca-Cola beverage operations are a fabulous money machine. Coca-Cola delivers the equivalent of 274 eight-ounce containers of beverage to every man, woman and child in the U.S.! Its business abroad is growing dramatically, and Coca-Cola controls over 30% of the soft-drink markets in Japan, West Germany, Argentina, Brazil and Mexico. Huge potential markets exist in China and India.

Coca-Cola's "outside" enterprises, however, have not been as successful. The entertainment sector needs upgrading, and Minute Maid frozen orange juice is meeting powerful competition from natural juice purveyor Tropicana. But Coke makes so much money in its main pursuit that it can easily support these less rewarding sectors.

This remarkably durable and successful company prospered from the start with its secret formula for "Coke." It has built a massive fountain trade and store distribution system through its unique bottle design and network of exclusive bottlers. Today, the company grosses over $9 billion annually, about 20% of which it converts into operating income. In recent years, foreign operations comprised 46% of sales and delivered 63% of operating income.

The company has been a rewarding equity for investors. It has paid continuous cash dividends since 1893 and distributed a 200% stock dividend in 1986 and a 100% stock dividend in 1987. Dividends have been increased for the last twelve years in a row. About half of the shares are owned by institutions.

Coca-Cola meets all the requirements for a Fortress Stock as the company continues its historic growth. As a consumer-type equity, Coca-Cola provides excellent representation in the beverage and entertainment industries.

COLGATE-PALMOLIVE COMPANY

■ ■ ■

NYSE Symbol: CL

This traditional consumer product company, with annual sales exceeding $5 billion, is a durable and attractive choice for long-term investment. It ranks as the second largest manufacturer and marketer of detergents, toiletries and staple brand-name household products.

An enumeration of its popular brands, which are well known worldwide, is most impressive. Among its cleansers are Fab, Fresh Start, Ajax, Dynamo and Palmolive. Toothpastes are Colgate and Ultra Brite. There are also Palmolive and Irish Spring soaps, Colgate shaving creams and Curad bandages. The company also produces industrial tapes, nonwoven fibers and pet foods.

Highlights of recent operations include the successful marketing of Colgate Tartar Control toothpaste, Palmolive Liquid dishwashing detergent and Fab One Shot, a unique detergent that combines a fabric softening element and a static-eliminating agent.

In 1988, Colgate-Palmolive began a substantial corporate restructuring program. It has arranged the sale of its health care subsidiary, Kendall, which should realize close to $1 billion. It has also sold off several uneconomic units. The company stresses cost controls at all levels of manufacture and marketing, and it has placed increased emphasis on foreign business, which delivered a little more than half its sales in recent years.

Another positive element for Colgate-Palmolive is the company's real estate holdings. Colgate owns extensive land and building properties in Jersey City, New Jersey, where rapid expansion of office buildings is taking place and land prices have soared.

The company is financially strong, with over $1.3 billion in working capital and little long-term debt. Property dispositions now in progress will expand working capital substantially and pave the way for (1) compatible acquisitions, (2) reduction of debt, (3) repurchase of shares, and (4) continued dividend increases.

The company is energetic in its pursuit of corporate progress and profitability. Net earnings have more than doubled in less than a decade. Dividends have been increased in each year since 1972 and should continue to rise. Managerial efficiency is illustrated by annual profits equal to 22% of net worth.

Colgate-Palmolive shares trade actively. There are over 69 million common shares outstanding, with sizable institutional holdings.

Colgate-Palmolive is definitely an attractive Fortress Stock. It has stature, a long record of increased earnings and profits, strong consumer franchises in many markets, a reputation for quality and a record of consistently rewarding production and marketing of new products. The shares have the further value of being recession resistant and of offsetting the cost of living by dividends enhanced yearly. Everything points to Colgate-Palmolive's ability to continue to maintain its quality status and investment desirability.

CONSOLIDATED EDISON COMPANY OF NEW YORK, INC.

■ ■ ■

NYSE Symbol: Ed

Consolidated Edison is one of the most successful utility companies in America. It supplies electricity throughout New York City and in most of Westchester County. Gas and steam are also supplied in parts of this broad metropolitan area.

Sales of electricity account for about 80% of revenues. Commercial and industrial use is about double that of residential use. Power production is balanced among oil, nuclear, gas and purchased sources. Rather than adding to its generation facilities, Con Ed is a steady purchaser of power from Canada and from the

New York State Power Pool. No new power stations will be needed until into the 1990s.

As the financial center of America, New York provides a strong economy with growing demand for utility services. It possesses a Public Service Commission that has been reasonably responsive to the company's requests for rate increases. This considerate regulatory climate has benefited Con Ed stockholders, generating dependable and frequently increased dividends.

The company is a massive corporation with gross properties worth over $10 billion, total invested capital of $8.2 billion and annual operating revenues of $5 billion.

The company has one of the best capital structures in the nation, divided as follows: 36.3% in long-term debt, 8.8% in preferred stock and 54.9% in common stocks. Institutions own 30% of the 134 million shares outstanding. It is company practice to pay out about 60% of earnings in yearly cash dividends.

For the income-minded, Con Ed is an attractive investment. The shares were split 2 for 1 in 1982. Cash dividends have been regularly increased in each year since 1976. This annual increase in dividends is an attractive feature and gives the shares some of the qualities of an inflation hedge. In common with seasoned utility shares, the company trades within a fairly narrow range.

The only cloud in the sky for Con Ed would seem to be the aftereffects of the October 1987 crash. New York employment is heavily concentrated in the financial industry—Wall Street, the big banks and insurance companies. If this industry becomes depressed and lays off tens of thousands of employees, then the long-term growth curve of the company might flatten out.

The history of New York, however, and its tradition as headquarters for the biggest banks and corporations in the country, make us confident that Con Ed will continue as a role model for flourishing institutions and continue to enhance the financial position of its shareholders. Regular dividend increases of 9% a year are nothing to be sneezed at.

We regard Consolidated Edison as a worthy holding in any well-structured portfolio, one that definitely qualifies as a Fortress Stock.

THE DOW CHEMICAL COMPANY

■ ■ ■

NYSE Symbol: Dow

Dow ranks as the second largest chemical company, with revenues of over $11 billion and $12.5 billion in assets. It benefits from one of the broadest and most integrated product lines in the industry and is upgrading its profits by converting the raw chemicals it controls into popular consumer products with worldwide acceptance.

Starting out with basic raw materials such as natural gas, crude oil, brine and benzine, Dow develops a broad product mix of derivatives. It benefits competitively by integration and "in-house" supply of the basic chemicals it needs.

Dow operates primarily through five product groups:

1. Ethylene derivatives, which account for about 17% of operating income
2. Styrene and by-products (20%)
3. Chlor-alkali and derivatives (20%)
4. Propylene oxide and derivatives (12%)
5. Pharmaceuticals (11%)

The rest of operating income is supplied by assorted specialty chemicals and fabricated products.

Dow ranks among the largest ethylene producers and uses 75% of its production internally. In styrene, Dow is one of the largest global producers, and applies 85% of production to its own use.

Dow is the number one U.S. producer in the chlor-alkali (chlorene and caustic soda) industry. Recent consolidation in this sector has reduced competition and given Dow a marketing edge.

Propylene oxides are strongly linked to consumer durables, although this sector is not growing as rapidly as other divisions.

A catalog of all these basics is rather arid, but the end use of these chemicals, as they are converted into consumer products, is more familiar.

In pharmaceuticals, Dow offers Seldane, a prescription antihistamine with $230 million in sales and a strong potential for increased volume. Other drugs include cough and cold preparations and antibiotics.

Consumer products include Handi-wrap, Saran Wrap, Ziplock bags and Fantastik cleaner. The company also has an excellent line of herbicides and insecticides.

More than half of sales come from foreign markets and thus benefit from the declining dollar.

Dow had documented its managerial competence by improving its profit margins and plant efficiency year after year. As a blue chip in its industry, Dow definitely merits inclusion in our list of Fortress Stocks. Dividends, continuously paid since 1911, were increased five times in the last decade. There are 191 million shares outstanding, and there is a current program to buy back a million shares in the market.

Dow offsets the rather cyclical nature of its business by steadily upgrading its products into higher-margin consumer products. It is on a steady profit upcurve. Dow provides the quality and diversity suitable for a Fortress holding. Ahead lie rising dividends, a stock split and contented share-owners.

DUN & BRADSTREET CORPORATION

■ ■ ■

NYSE Symbol: DNB

In the quest for companies dominant in their industries, we have identified Dun & Bradstreet as a long-term winner, with a long history of rising profits and dividends. Dun & Bradstreet is a broad-based business service organization, and the leading publisher of business information.

The American economy is built on credit, and Dun & Bradstreet is a major source of credit information, domestically and worldwide. It reports and rates credit standings and it supplies sales and financial data, computer software and database services. It can instantly deliver a credit report on hundreds of thousands of corporations.

The publishing business of Dun & Bradstreet is less well publicized. The stable of publishing companies includes Official Air Line Guides, a publisher of reference guides for the airlines industry, and Reuben H. Donnelley, a major publisher of telephone directories. There is also Moody's Investor Services, which supplies those fat manuals on securities found in every broker's office, as well as offers guidance to investors with its quarterly ratings on bonds of all kinds. A Business Education and Services division offers correspondence courses and runs business seminars.

In marketing services, Dun & Bradstreet is a versatile leader with its Donnelley Marketing Services. Nielsen Marketing (the bible on measuring television program viewing) is supplemented by Nielsen Media Research and Clearing House. Added to these are Data Quest and Neodata Services direct marketing, market planning sales promotion and circulation fulfillment services, domestic and foreign.

In early 1988, Dun & Bradstreet announced an agreement to buy I.M.S. International for $1.77 billion in stock. I.M.S. specializes in market research and database publishing services to pharmaceutical companies. I.M.S. earned $44.6 million in 1987 on revenues of $411.5 million.

These components, as sketched above, constitute an innovative and aggressive rapidly growing company with over $3.3 billion gross annually and with total assets in the same range. While these operating units may appear a bit sprawling, each unit is designed as an ably-managed profit center. The end result is a solid company that regularly increases its revenues, profits and dividends year after year. To illustrate, in the past ten years earnings per share have risen every year (except 1983), and are now five times higher than a decade ago. Dividends, paid continuously since 1934, were increased each year since 1977 and are five times higher since that year. Along the way there were 100% stock dividends in 1983 and 1987.

The company has 152 million shares now outstanding, and there is no debt. Here is a Fortress Stock that will truly let you sleep at night.

EXXON CORPORATION

■ ■ ■

NYSE Symbol: XON

Energy stocks will be among the outstanding performers in the next three years. Low crude prices in 1987 and 1988 have generally discouraged new drilling, so that when oil prices return to $30 or higher, companies such as Exxon with vast reserves will prosper mightily. Royal Dutch and Exxon represent the "Class" of the international oils and both belong on our Fortress list.

Exxon (formerly Standard Oil of New Jersey) has the distinction of being the world's largest petroleum company. Its reserves of crude and natural gas liquids were 7,354 million barrels and 46.3 billion cubic feet of natural gas. Quite a stockpile!

Further, the company is completely integrated, from exploration and production to refining, transportation and marketing. These operations are supplemented by major chemical and coal productions.

Aggressive reduction in overhead and a sloughing-off of nonprofitable assets in 1987–88 streamlined operations and released funds for major acquisitions. To illustrate, in 1987, Exxon spent $650 million to take over Celeron (from Goodyear Tire), adding millions of barrels of crude to reserves. Next, Exxon laid out $680 million to buy Delhi Petroleum, Ltd., a major Australian producer. Delhi has 25% of Australia's biggest offshore oil yield. Exxon has huge oil stores all around the world and plans a further allocation of $7 billion for capital and exploration outlays.

Revenues are massive—over $70 billion a year. Profits have been in a steady uptrend, earnings per share rising fourfold over the last ten years. Exxon has been generous in distributions to share-owners, paying out about 50% of net earnings in cash dividends, with 100% stock dividends in 1981 and in 1987.

There are about 1.4 billion common shares outstanding. Exxon has been a favored core holding for individuals because of its above-average cash dividend (paid continuously since 1882), its sterling market performance and the well-documented efficiency of its management.

While others have neglected oil exploration and drilling, Exxon, as we have noted, has been shrewdly adding to its crude holdings in order to feed its refineries for years to come and to greatly expand its earning power when crude prices move up past $20.

Exxon is a Fortress Stock that lets you sleep—and prosper!

FORD MOTOR COMPANY

■ ■ ■

NYSE Symbol: F

Ford Motor Company has made outstanding progress in recent years, accounting now for over 20% of the U.S. motor car market and 30% of the light truck market. Ford reported larger profits than GM in 1987 and 1988. We have therefore designated Ford as one of our choice thirty Fortress Stocks.

With annual sales in the $70 billion range and assets of over $40 billion, Ford has achieved enviable stature. More particularly, it has a remarkable cash flow and vast resources enabling it to finance expanded operations internally, finance prudent acquisitions, permit substantial repurchase of its own shares and increase dividends.

About 60% of Ford net income flows from profits on U.S. and Canadian production of cars and trucks, 24% from overseas operations, and the balance from income from financial subsidiaries in North America. Ford has operated profitably in Europe since 1978.

The big point for investors to consider is the cash flow generated by Ford. According to our estimate, Ford cash flow from operations, over and above capital outlays and dividends paid, could exceed $3 billion a year in 1989 and future years, which could fund generous dividend increases. While the motor industry is cyclical, Ford operates with such efficiency as to flatten out the swings and to assure dependable and rising dividends in the years ahead.

Ford is now the standout automotive stock within the Big Three and is best equipped to generate cash flow, increase its dividend and retire common stock (which can increase the value of the stock outstanding). Ford shares make a logical appeal to all investors who believe in concentrating on a fundamentally sound stock with a bright future.

KELLOGG COMPANY

■ ■ ■

NYSE Symbol: K

It would be hard to find a more classic consumer product company than Kellogg. Its name is a household word around the world, and its product line features the most famous breakfast foods. It is the outstanding American producer of ready-to-eat cereals. It also derives a third of its gross from foreign operations.

Popular name brands under the Kellogg flag include Corn Flakes, Rice Krispies, Special K, All Bran, Raisin Bran, Apple Jacks, Product 19 and others. Non-cereal products include stuffing croutons, salad dressings, baking mixes and syrups.

In another food sector, there is Mrs. Smith's Frozen Foods, maker of frozen desserts, pies and waffles. In addition, the Salada Food division offers teas and desserts. Miscellaneous foods include soups, gelatins, pie bases and entrees prepared for restaurants. Less known perhaps are Whitney's yogurts.

Kellogg is dominant in its field, accounting for over 40% of the U.S. ready-to-eat cereal market. It thrives not only on the steady sales of its traditional and long established foods but on its ability to create, promote and market with great vigor new products in a savagely competitive marketplace. In addition to its skill at product origination, Kellogg has shrewdly acquired compatible lines that have broadened company markets while maintaining profit margins.

Proof of managerial capability is evidenced by the consistent growth in revenues—from over $1.5 billion in 1977 to over $3.5 billion currently. In the same period, earnings per share have almost quadrupled.

Investors generally have not paid sufficient attention to Kellogg, perhaps because 34% of it is locked up in the Kellogg Trust. The shares, however, enjoy an active market, supported by a $100 million allocation of funds to repurchase stock.

Kellogg has been around long enough to prove thoroughly dependable, an excellent performer in good times and recessions, with increased annual dividends for thirty-two years in a row. These assets are proper attributes of Fortress-type stocks.

Steadily expanding global markets, effective cost controls, a lower tax rate and a declining dollar are additional profit-building factors in this picture. The company has over $2 billion in total corporate assets. Who could ask for anything more in a first-rate **Fortress Stock?**

MARRIOTT CORPORATION

■ ■ ■

NYSE Symbol: MHS

Marriott is at the head of the class in the lodging industry. It is the largest manager and operator of hotels in the world, a leader in contract food services and a major franchiser of restaurant chains. Hotel operations represent about half of Marriott's total earnings and have fueled a remarkable earnings-per-share growth rate: 21% annually since 1970!

The company now has 48 franchised hotels with a total of almost 16,000 rooms. The remaining hotels in the system (127, with over 61,000 rooms) are operated by Marriott. Of these, 19 are owned and 108 are under long contracts. Franchise fees may deliver 4% of a hotel's room sales, while management fees may be 9% of total sales, including room, food and beverage.

The entire Hotel Group includes the owned hotels and three newer chains. The moderately priced chains, Courtyard Inn and Residence Inn, are being expanded at the rate of about forty a year, with Residence Inn featuring a relatively new development in the trade—the concept of extended stay. The third and newest chain, Fairfield Inn, is an economy-oriented group and is still being tested before any aggressive expansion takes place. Two have been opened so far.

In addition, Marriott is a leading supplier of contract food services, handling the food catering for over two thousand businesses, medical care and educational institutions. This sector was notably expanded by the acquisition in 1986 of Saga Corporation for about $700 million.

The third facet of Marriott's operations is restaurants. The chain includes Roy Rogers fast foods (300 company-operated and 209 franchised units) and Big Boy (202 owned and 707 franchised). In addition, there are 152 restaurant units and 190 Howard Johnson outlets that Marriott either divested or converted.

Lodging contributes over half of the company's profits, contract foods a third, and restaurants contribute the balance.

Marriott hotels feature high-quality service and well-managed licensees. Occupancy in Marriott hotels is about ten percentage points over the industry average. Median room rates in 1987 were about $90.

Marriott leads the industry in quality, status and profitability, an element we stress in Fortress Stocks. Here is a company that has increased its profits and dividends each year in the past decade. Earnings per share rose well over fivefold in the last decade and are expected to continue rising. Revenues are expected to grow by 12% this year.

We expect Marriott to continue to outperform the DJIA and Standard & Poor's 500. The company has 119 million shares outstanding. There was a 400% stock dividend in 1986.

Marriott is an elite equity with a rich real estate base. It is certainly one of the more dynamic Fortress selections.

MARSH & McLENNAN COMPANIES, INC.

■ ■ ■

NYSE Symbol: MMC

Marsh & McLennan, a holding company, is the world leader in insurance brokerage and conducts an extensive re-insurance business as well, with 65% of its revenues derived from its insurance operation. The company has paid a cash dividend continuously since 1923. In the insurance brokerage field, Marsh & McLennan acts as the agent for corporations and individuals in the selection of appropriate property and casualty coverage, as well as group life. The company not only selects the best underwriters, securing favorable rates for its clients, but also represents its clients in claim settlements.

Marsh & McLennan is international in scope, with clients and sponsored group programs in Canada and in the United Kingdom as well as in the United States.

Significant in any analysis of Marsh & McLennan is its mutual funds subsidiary, The Putnam Group, with $33 billion of assets under management. Other subsidiaries include Mercer Meidinger, an employee benefits consulting operation. With offices in nineteen countries, it is a global leader in this field. Recent tax and regulatory changes, as well as rising pressure for group health coverage, are rapidly expanding the employee benefits business in the United States.

Some other Marsh & McLennan subsidiaries are Guy Carpenter & Company and Bowring (two insurance services); Temple Barber and Stone, corporate strategy consultants; Clayton Environmental Consultants, who provide timely guidance in handling environmental risks; and Lippincott & Margulies, who develop various corporate identity and communication programs.

Marsh & McLennan has grown steadily in volume and stature. Annual revenues have risen from $475 million in 1978 to over $2 billion in 1988, and net earnings advanced in eight out of the past ten years. About 50% of net earnings is customarily paid out in cash. Cash dividends were increased in each of the past ten years and the cash dividend is now close to four times higher than it was a decade ago.

The company clearly qualifies as a Fortress Stock on its record and in its prospects. It is a seasoned specialist at the top of its field. Although the insurance brokerage business is highly competitive, Marsh & McLennan, as noted, has shown consistent growth. It is now generating new business at the rate of about 12% a year. In an economy threatened by inflation, corporations need to increase their property and casualty coverage substantially. Marsh & McLennan is strategically placed to profit from this trend. Moreover, its regularly increased annual dividends provide its stockholders with some offset to the rising cost of living.

THE MAY DEPARTMENT STORES COMPANY

■ ■ ■

NYSE Symbol: MA

May Department Stores has established itself as the leading department store retailer in America. It steadily improved its merchandising and productivity in the early 1980s and attained its present stature by merger, in 1986, with Associated Department Stores.

The May Stores grossed $10.58 billion in fiscal 1987, with department stores divided among seventeen divisions. Well-known units include Lord & Taylor (New York), May Company California (Los Angeles and San Diego), Hecht's (Washington, D.C.), Famous Barr (St. Louis), Kaufmann's (Pittsburgh), Fox's

91

(Hartford), Goldwater's (Arizona), Hahne's (New Jersey), and others.

Discount stores include the Caldor chain, with 115 stores in Northeastern states, and Venture stores with 65 units in the Midwest.

Specialty merchandising is conducted by Volume Shoes, a self-service shoe chain with over 2,200 stores. And, most recently acquired, there is Loehmann's off-price women's apparel with ninety outlets.

May has extensive real estate operations related to retailing, with five owned shopping centers and partnerships in twenty-two others.

May has long been respected for the quality of its management, and the company is constantly at work to improve efficiency by opening new stores, renovating and phasing out uneconomic units. A key statistic is sales per gross square feet per year. This figure has risen 30% in the past five years.

Expansion is steadily underway, with 59 department stores and some 1,300 specialty stores scheduled to open over the four-year period 1986–1990.

Efficient buying is a major ingredient in May's retailing. This is done through May Merchandising Corporation in New York, which works closely with the regional stores in maintaining an inventory that can be turned over rapidly and that anticipates customers' demand in the various geographical areas serviced. To create and maintain loyal customer patronage, May stresses "friendliness" on the part of its sales personnel.

The company has doubled earnings per share in

the last four years. Earnings are expected to continue to grow at 15% compounded through 1992, with a return on equity averaging above 15%. Dividends, paid since 1911, have increased every year in the past decade.

May shares merit Fortress classification. We expect May to move well on its own initiative, although it might also prove attractive to an acquisitor.

McDONALD'S CORPORATION

■ ■ ■

NYSE Symbol:MCD

McDonald's is a remarkable company, grossing over $5 billion a year, with earnings growing at the annual rate of 15%. It is the dominant company in the restaurant and fast food industry, serving a fantastic 20 million customers a day. It is constantly broadening its base by the shrewd introduction of new products, such as McNuggets, prepackaged salads, croissants and the like.

McDonald's is also an international company. It has 2,340 restaurants abroad, which generate $3.5 billion in annual sales and employ 29% of corporate assets. Foreign operations are projected to grow at the rate of 25% annually. About 40% of its new store openings are scheduled abroad.

McDonald's owns 59% of the nearly ten thousand restaurants in its global network, making the company a huge corporate landlord. Thus, earnings are derived not just from profits from owned restaurants and licensed operations but also from rental revenues, which are geared to, and expand with, sales. The rent on franchised outlets is set at 8.5% of each outlet's sales, and this percentage is moving higher. Imagine the growth potential of rentals alone when McDonald's opens a new restaurant somewhere in the world every seventeen hours! Seventy-six percent of restaurants are franchised, and there is a waiting list of twenty thousand applications for new franchises.

McDonald's is an aggressive advertiser and the McDonald's logo is one of the best known of American trademarks. The impact of McDonald's advertising seems definitely more impressive and productive than its competitors, including Howard Johnson and Wendy's.

McDonald's is consistently profitable. It has reported 7.5 years of continuous growth. Earnings per share are expected to continue an upward trend. The management has a continuing program for increased efficiency—ultra-modern new equipment and further computerization. The company generates a 20% return on equity, much higher than most restaurant chains.

There are almost 190 million shares outstanding, and the shares are popular with institutions.

McDonald's has moved solidly into the investment scene in the past five years and its shares have now attained investment grade. McDonald's is regarded as a durable stock in an essential industry and a worthy Fortress portfolio holding, especially for those who stress growth more than income.

MERCK & COMPANY

■ ■ ■

NYSE Symbol: MRK

Merck is the standout company in the drug industry. It ranks among the largest drug firms in the world,
with an outstanding record for researching new products, for testing and getting them approved by the
Federal Drug Administration (FDA) and for highly
profitable global marketing.

Analysts of the drug industry attribute the progress
of Merck in recent years to the genius of president Roy
Vagelos. Since about 50% of its sales are from the
international market, Merck has benefited greatly from
the devalued dollar. Merck's profits rose 67% in the last
couple of years and are now over $900 million annually.

99

Profits have risen from established pharmaceutical formulations and from an impressive group of new products. Here are some of the winners: Aldomet and Vasotec, hypertensives; Clinoril and Indocin, anti-inflammatory medicines; Meloxin, an antibiotic; Timoptic for glaucoma; and Mevacor for lowering cholesterol. Mevacor is remarkable for its approval by the FDA, granted within ten months' time rather than the two to three years it usually takes for approval. These and dozens of lesser-known vaccines, biologicals and psychotherapeutics have contributed to push sales well over the $4 billion mark.

Merck also has two specialty chemical divisions, which account for about 5% of its annual profits: Calgon Corporation, a specialist in water treatment, and the Kelco division, producer of paints, paper and cleansing products.

The secret of success at Merck lies in its research and development program, with a typical one-year outlay of over $500 million, the largest bankroll for research in the industry. Merck develops its new products mainly in-house, rather than by licensing, a policy that generates higher profit margins.

In recent years, Merck has been among the most popular drug companies on Wall Street, even though it has the highest-priced stock. Investors and analysts are thoroughly impressed with the financial strength of the company.

To illustrate, net income has been moving up at the rate of over 30% a year recently. Further, earnings per share are also in a strong upturn. These earnings are buttressed by a strong balance sheet, with working capital of over $1.1 billion and very little debt.

Confidence in the company is also justified by the dividend record. Cash dividends, paid since 1935, have been boosted in each of the past eleven years. Merck presently pays a dividend five times higher than it did a decade ago. Earnings more than justify this upward progression.

In any diversified list of top-flight equities, Merck should find a place. It is suggested as a **Fortress Stock** without any reservations.

MINNESOTA MINING AND MANUFACTURING COMPANY

■ ■ ■

NYSE Symbol: MMM

This high-quality and recession-resistant company easily merits inclusion among our thirty Fortress Stocks. Its capacity for growth and gain have been well documented for eighty-five years, and the company continues its forward motion at an enviable pace.

Minnesota Mining and Manufacturing, otherwise known as "3M," has prospered by innovation, by technology and by carving out niches in an expanding series of rewarding markets. It pioneered in waterproof sandpaper in 1920, became famous for Scotch tape and its many profitable applications, pioneered Thinsulate (energy control film for windows) and developed an array of pharmaceuticals and agricultural chemicals. It

103

even expanded into the field of digital sound recording. The efficiency, technological superiority and breadth of the 3M product line have led to continuous expansion of sales and profits. Its product acceptance is, of course, worldwide. Managerial competence has consistently generated high returns on equity and outstanding after-tax margins.

Despite its present size and stature, the company continues to follow its programmed targets: 10% annual growth in profits, return on capital of above 25%; 20% return on equity; and 25% of each year's sales total derived from recently introduced (within the past five years) products. Important to this progress is an aggressive research and development program.

3M now gets 40% of its sales from business overseas, and aims to increase this figure to 50% by more aggressive penetration of target markets.

Through the regular introduction of functional new products carrying high profit margins, and by widening its sales horizons, the company has reported consistently higher earnings year after year. Since 1945, the only "down" years were 1975, 1982 and 1985. This is a company of significant stature, grossing $9 billion a year.

The company has over 220 million shares outstanding. The stock is quite attractive in view of 3M's long and consistent performance as a growth company, high profit margins, the steady flow of new products to market and a rock-solid balance sheet. Few would question 3M's qualifications as a Fortress Stock.

J.P. MORGAN & COMPANY

■ ■ ■

NYSE Symbol: JPM

Morgan is the most distinguished name in American banking. J.P. Morgan & Company, parent of Morgan Guaranty Trust Company, is a banking institution of stature and belongs, as a core holding, in any balanced portfolio of elite equities.

Apart from its name, what's so wonderful about Morgan? For one thing, it has been a consistently top performer in its field in the percentage of its earnings on equity. Further, its capital-to-assets ratio is 6%, much higher than other money-centered banks. Other majors in this field—Citicorp and Manufacturers Hanover—had to increase their capital by public offering of new shares in 1987. J.P. Morgan did not. Its 180 million shares are sufficient and should continue to remain undiluted.

J.P. Morgan enjoys a top franchise in wholesale and investment banking. Its unique nature and penetration of the market among first-quality international corporations and governments have created a clientele of the highest caliber. Its banking products are progressive, innovative and profitable. It is strong in personal trusts and manages billions in investment portfolios. In addition to the traditional facilities of banking and trust functions, the company offers capital restructuring, Euro-bond financing, foreign exchange, merger and acquisition consultation, and financial guidance. Morgan management is regarded as among the most sophisticated in the industry. Further, Morgan is poised to take advantage of any new deregulation of banking, such as the underwriting of securities and interstate banking.

The company balances wholesale lending with a substantial bond portfolio, supervised by seasoned professionals. Its judgment in portfolio management has been notable, especially after the October 1987 debacle, when, in contrast with the stock market, the bond market moved sharply forward.

In common with other money-centered banks, Morgan had made extensive loans to the less-developed countries. As these loans deteriorated, the bank was among the first to "bite the bullet," taking a 25% writeoff in this loan sector in 1987. Moreover, Morgan evidences little exposure to realty loans, has not become heavily involved in leveraged buyout financing, and the large business it does with brokerage firms is well protected by collateral.

Morgan has justified its inclusion in our list of Fortress Stocks because of its long record of profitability and continuous cash dividend payment since 1892, buttressed by stock dividends and a rewarding issue of convertible bonds. We believe J.P. Morgan & Company will maintain its leadership and benefit its shareowners by steadily expanding earnings and dividends in future years.

MOTOROLA, INC.

■ ■ ■

NYSE Symbol: MOT

We have done considerable research on companies in the electronics and communications business and have rejected the obvious role models—General Electric and IBM—as companies already super-mature and with less potential for future forward motion. Conversely, our studies indicate that Motorola has special merit as a Fortress Stock. We find our judgment supported by the inclusion of Motorola in several major stock mutual funds.

Motorola is a major producer of semiconductor products essential in electronic communications and in two-way radios. It is also preeminent in data communications and information systems. It has recently aligned itself with IBM in a special joint effort in these fields.

Motorola has been a leader in making two-way radios and paging systems. It is also a major factor in integration and memory circuits, microprocessors and linear and logic circuits.

In addition, the company features a broad line of information system products, including such strange-sounding items as high-speed modems, multiplexers and digital interface units, all essential devices for computer consoles.

Furthermore, a big sector of Motorola's business is in government electronics sales. Their product line also includes automotive products and complete mobile telephone systems.

Motorola has grown and prospered in all of these technological areas, thanks to a reputation for quality production and innovative research, leading to significant new product introductions. Management seeks to be in the mainstream of advance in high-growth areas and in the ever-expanding computer industry. Sales are now over $6 billion a year. Foreign markets now provide over 30% of sales and benefit from the declining dollar.

Motorola is more cyclical than some of the stocks cited but appears desirable both because of the dynamics of the economic sectors served and because of its rapidly rising profitability.

Motorola stock has shown a rising trend since 1981. It has increased cash dividends five times in the past ten years. There was a 200% stock dividend in 1984. Finances are strong, with over $900 million in working capital and a low long-term debt. Institutions own 65% of the over 128 million shares outstanding.

Motorola is an honored name and a solid Fortress Stock for patient retention.

NYNEX
CORPORATION

■ ■ ■

NYSE Symbol: NYN

NYNEX is the choice representative in the communications sector of public utilities. It is the most dynamic of the seven regional operating telephone companies that were part of AT&T until 1984, when AT&T was forced to split off the seven current regional telephone companies.

NYNEX is a massive enterprise with $25 billion in assets and annual revenues of $12 billion. It is the second largest telephone holding company, providing, through its subsidiaries (New York Telephone Company and New England Telephone and Telegraph), telecommunication and access service in New York and the six New England states through more than 14 million customer access lines. Over 50% of revenues are generated in the New York and Boston metropolitan areas.

NYNEX is rapidly expanding its mobile communications services (NYNEX Mobile) and, through its NYNEX Business Centers, offers a variety of telecommunication and information systems. NYNEX also provides management, supplies, warehouse, servicing and repairs for the area, as well as international marketing and consulting services.

NYNEX shares ownership of Bell Communication Research, which, with the six other regional phone companies, carries on the vital research and development services that were part of the original Bell system.

Many factors point to long-term expansion at NYNEX: the rapid growth of the New York and New England areas, a region of minimum unemployment; the new cellular telephone services; completely redesigned phone systems, computer-compatible for offices and entire companies; and improved fiber optic transmissions.

In balanced portfolios today, a reasonable percentage of holdings is customarily allocated to telephone and electric utilities because they are defensive securities. A defensive security is one that is more stable than average and provides a safe return (dependable dividends) on an investor's money. When the stock market is weak, defensive securities tend to decline less than the overall market.

NYNEX is a good value, with sturdy defensive characteristics. Telephone use continues during recessions and is a remarkably dependable source of corporate cash flow.

NYNEX has over 200 million shares outstanding, about 35% of which are institutionally held. The company is a generous dividend payer. Cash dividends have been paid regularly and increased since 1984. In addition, there was a 100% stock dividend in 1986. This is indeed a fully qualified Fortress Stock.

POTOMAC ELECTRIC POWER

■ ■ ■

NYSE Symbol: POM

Potomac Electric Power is one of the most attractive electric utilities in the United States by virtue of the territory it serves, its growth rate, its dividend record and its horizons for future progress.

Potomac supplies electricity to the District of Columbia and adjacent areas of Maryland. This Washington metropolitan district is one of the most stable and prosperous areas of the country, uniquely insulated from recession by the absence of cyclical industrial operations. The population served is 1.8 million and growing, at the hub of government operations that, whether under Republicans or Democrats, are unlikely to diminish.

Classification of Potomac's revenues by customer demand is unique: residential, 27%; commercial, 49%; federal government, 16%; miscellaneous, 8%.

Power generation is more than adequate from existing stations by prudent adjustment of load factors and by arrangements for purchasing additional power. A new coal-gasification plant is in the planning stage, scheduled to operate in the middle 1990s. Investors also favor Potomac because it does not rely on nuclear power: its fuels are 88% coal and 12% oil.

In common with other progressive utilities, Potomac Electric Power has a subsidiary for the development of nonregulated investments, Potomac Capital Investments, with current assets of $520 million, including a balanced portfolio of tax-sheltered mutual funds and preferred stocks (income 85% tax-exempt). This unit is also expanding into equipment leasing. It makes a significant contribution to corporate earnings.

Annual operating revenues have increased steadily, rising from $1 billion to over $1.4 billion over the last six years. Earnings per share have risen at an even faster rate, doubling during the same period, with dividends expanding in that period by 60%. Cash dividends have been paid continuously since 1904, and there was a 100% stock dividend in 1987.

Utility analysts have given a top rating to Potomac Electric Power because of its consistent record of growth and gain, cash flow, and long history of annual dividend increases. The half-billion-dollar capital investment company is another bonus.

A possible criticism of Potomac is that it does not yield quite as much as other utilities, such as Con Edison or Baltimore Gas & Electric. But in our view the slightly lower yield on Potomac is more than offset by quality of earnings, balance of its financial structure and legitimate expectations for regular dividend increases. Potomac Electric Power definitely belongs on our list of Fortress Stocks.

PROCTOR & GAMBLE COMPANY

■ ■ ■

NYSE Symbol: PG

One of the most renowned consumer product companies in the world is Proctor & Gamble, with almost
170 million shares outstanding. These shares are a
long-term core holding in the portfolios of conservative
individual investors as well as institutions, which own
44% of the stock.

Proctor & Gamble, a global corporation, is the leading household and personal care products company. It
has displayed steady growth for decades, both through
the development of new foods and beverages and by a
series of acquisitions that have diversified corporate

operations, enchanced earning power and provided profit stability.

We could not begin to cover here the vast number of products of Proctor & Gamble; they are recognized around the world as household products in the kitchen, laundry and medicine closet. Laundry and personal care products together generate about 80% of sales.

Laundry products include Bounce, Cheer, Cascade, Ivory Snow and Ivory liquid. Cleaning products include Mr. Clean, Downey, Comet and Spic and Span. Well-known personal care products include Ivory, Zest and Camay bar soaps; Bounty paper towel; Charmin and White Cloud bathroom tissue; Pampers and LUV disposable diapers; Sure and Secret deodorants; Crest, a leading toothpaste; Head & Shoulders, Prell and Vidal Sassoon for hair care; and Oil of Olay for skin care. In the health care field there is the Vicks line of cold and cough medicines.

Brand-name food leaders are also familiar: Folgers coffee, Tenderleaf tea, Crisco, Duncan Hines cake mixes, Jif peanut butter, Pringles potato chips, and the beverages Crush, Hines and Citrus Hill juices.

These are among the best known products. Disposable diapers are the leader in volume, accounting for about 16% of sales.

In 1987, Proctor & Gamble acquired Blandax, Germany's major toothpaste maker. Important recent acquisitions are Richardson Vicks, Inc., and G.D. Searles in proprietary drugs.

Research and development are vital keys to future profits. New products in the pipeline are a prescription drug for ulcers, a hair-growth product (developed jointly with Upjohn), and Olestra, a new calorie-free fat product useful in cooking and in a variety of foods that use oils and shortenings. As these come on the market, new horizons of profit will be opened up.

Dividends have increased every year since 1977 and have been paid without interruption since 1891. Annual revenues have expanded in the last decade from $9.3 billion to over $18 billion.

The owner of shares of Proctor & Gamble has good reason for being content with the stature, growing earnings and dividends of this company. Its broad diversity of consumer products insulates the company from cyclical swings, and the eminence of Proctor & Gamble in research, promotion and marketing of new products augurs well for the future.

Proctor & Gamble is a durable and desirable investment. It would be difficult to quarrel with its inclusion as a prime Fortress Stock.

ROYAL DUTCH PETROLEUM

■ ■ ■

NYSE Symbol: RD

Royal Dutch Petroleum is a massive international oil enterprise with over $46 billion in assets and a common stock of highest quality. Royal Dutch is a holding company owning 60% of the Royal Dutch/Shell Group. The other 40% is owned by Shell Trading & Transport Company, also publicly held.

The Group represents the second largest company in the global oil industry. Its operations are comprehensive, embracing production, transportation, refining and marketing. People think of the Royal Dutch/Shell Group mainly as a producer and processor of crude. Indeed, the Group crude supplies recently averaged over five million barrels a day. At 1986 year-end, reserves of the Group stood at 7,788 million barrels of crude and natural gas liquids, and refinery processing was at a sales ratio of 3.2 million barrels a day. Crude reserves are held all over the world—Norway, North America, Persian Gulf, Syria, Egypt, Oman and elsewhere.

In natural gas, the Group has the best worldwide position among its competitors. Recent natural gas sales were 6.2 million cubic feet per day, derived primarily from gas fields in the Netherlands and Brunei.

The Group excels in refining and marketing, with a modern refinery system, diversity of operations and depth in marketing resources. Worldwide recognition of the Shell logo is a definite asset. Retailing benefits in the United States from Shell Oil (100% owned) and Arco stations and abroad in Scandinavia and through Shell Oil of Canada (79% owned).

The Group also operates in coal and metals. In addition, chemicals delivered about $1 billion in net income in the past year.

The Group functions through more than 100 companies worldwide. It collects its income in sterling and distributes this income (also in sterling) to the owners: 60% to Royal Dutch and 40% to Shell Transport. Royal Dutch dividends are paid to British share-owners in pounds and to American share-owners in dollars.

Generous dividends have been paid continuously since 1947. Royal Dutch refining and marketing benefits from the lower dollar, which also increases the dividend to U.S. stockholders. Royal Dutch is a "class act" Fortress Stock for confident retention.

SCHLUMBERGER LTD.

■ ■ ■

NYSE Symbol: SLB

Schlumberger is the world's largest, most technically advanced oil service company. Most of the substantial oil wells in the world depend on this company for equipment, devices or services. Schlumberger so dominates the technical areas of oil production that it can prosper even without a strong recovery in global oil-field operations.

Schlumberger is the recognized leader in providing special drilling services and computerized wireline and interpretation services to the petroleum industry. When wells are drilled, they are logged to report and record progress and potentials. Schlumberger provides these logging services through mobile laboratories, electronically equipped to measure and define below-ground geological features. It dominates the world market on wireline services. This makes transmission of data to the surface possible without stopping drilling. Under development at Schlumberger is a new state-of-the-art generation of wireline equipment for more efficient well analysis and completion. This upcoming project opens a new horizon for growth and profit margins in years ahead.

Other facets of the company's operations include well testing and workover, seismic data, well cementing and stimulation, and offshore and land drilling, using ninety of its own rigs.

Schlumberger Industries is a division that makes meters and electric power distribution equipment, water meters, computer-aided design and manufacturing systems, and a variety of measurement instruments. This division contributes approximately 40% of revenues.

Schlumberger is included among our Fortress Stocks because of its semi-monopoly status in the most important technological areas in the oil business, as well as the profit potentials of its coming advanced line of wireline service, its profit uptrend, and an indicated growth rate of 12% annually.

The company has been an excellent earner, with 1986 the only slack year in a decade, caused by a decline in operating oil rigs and a non-recurring loss of $220 million from discontinued operations. It has $2 billion in working capital and very little debt.

Schlumberer is not as well known as some of our other Fortress Stocks, but its balance sheet, technological products and dependable income flow, as well as its potential for dividend increases, point to a most rewarding return.

THE SEAGRAM COMPANY, LTD.

■ ■ ■

NYSE Symbol: VO

The Seagram Company has been selected for the list of Fortress Stocks because it is the world's largest producer of distilled spirits and wines and has major representation in the chemical and oil industries through its 22.6% interest in Du Pont. Since 1981, the earnings curve has been steadily upward and dividends have been increased in nine out of the past ten years.

In alcoholic beverages, Seagram markets about 190 brands of distilled spirits and over 150 brands of wines, ports, sherries, champagnes and brandies in 205 countries. The company has operating affiliates or subsidiaries in twenty-seven nations.

Supplementing its dominance in the alcoholic beverage industry, Seagram owns 54.3 million shares (22.6%) of Du Pont de Nemours & Company, the largest manufacturer of chemicals in the United States and the creator of Orlon, Dacron, Nylon and other major synthetics. In addition, Du Pont is a significant factor in petroleum through its 100% ownership of Conoco, Inc., the ninth largest American oil company. Through dividends paid and through earnings, Seagram derived over $300 million in net income from Du Pont for the current year. Du Pont is one of the thirty companies that make up the Dow Jones Industrial Average. Its earnings per share rose over 16% in the last year.

In 1987 Seagram announced its intention to purchase Martell, a leading name in cognac. This goes well, on a quality basis, with Seagram's existing ownership of Mumm's champagne and Chivas Regal, a leading brand of Scotch whisky. Brandies represent the fastest-growing sector of the liquor trade around the world: demand is growing 15% a year, for example, in Hong Kong, Singapore and Malaysia.

As for diversification, Seagram's $7 billion in assets include 1.4 trillion cubic feet of proven natural gas reserves in the Gulf of Thailand.

Seagram's custom is to increase dividends regularly in response to higher earnings. There was a 200% stock dividend in 1983. (Seagram is a Canadian company, but all figures here are in U.S. dollars.)

Seagram is a fairly active issue on the New York Stock Exchange. We think it is poised for enhancement in value, due to, among other factors, the improving profitability of Du Pont and the prudent addition of Martell.

The Seagram Company has a place on our list because of its diversification in beverages, chemicals and oil and because of its Fortress-type balance sheet with over $1.5 billion in working capital. Forty percent of the stock is held by the Bronfman family, heirs of the original founder, Sam Bronfman.

TRI-CONTINENTAL CORPORATION

■ ■ ■

NYSE Symbol: TY

This is our one excursion into investment trusts. An investment trust invests pooled funds of individual investors in a group of selected securities and, like a corporation, has a fixed number of outstanding shares that are traded like stock. Tri-Continental has been selected to round out our Fortress portfolio because it is dedicated to the same kind of quality blue-chip performance that makes up our Fortress list. It is also one of the oldest closed-end trusts, having been in business for almost sixty years. Its shares are actively traded on the New York Stock Exchange, and in several years its

135

cash dividends have provided the most generous yields of any stock issues on the Exchange.

Tri-Continental is a stock-oriented, closed-end investment trust with assets of $1.25 billion. Its portfolio of about $1 billion in common stocks is diversified in about eighty selected issues. Its largest holding is Dow Chemical, representing $70 million market value.

This fund is ably managed and seeks not only dependable income but opportunities for capital gain that may present themselves through short-term swings in the market. Investment in Tri-Continental gives Fortress holders an opportunity to share specifically in this kind of trading gain made by a competent group of investment professionals. (Elsewhere I have, as you may have noted, downgraded short-run trading by individuals as being, in general, unproductive and diversive.)

Tri-Continental pays out two kinds of dividends: a pro-rata share of dividends and interest collected regularly and a year-end distribution of market gains realized. Some of these gains have been sizable—from 15% to over 20%. On Tri-Continental's latest annual distribution, the shares yielded 20.4%. Such a high return is especially attractive to senior or retired people whose other stock holdings may yield only 5% or 6%.

One feature attraction of Tri-Continental is that dividends may be delivered in stock, to steadily increase one's holdings, or taken in cash. Stock accumulation is particularly attractive for IRA funds. Many share-owners switch from stock payments to cash distributions when they enter retirement years.

The inclusion of Tri-Continental is justified by the quality of their portfolio, a respectable record of sagacious management over a period of many years and low operating expenses. Its yield record makes Tri-Continental especially worthwhile as a Fortress portfolio component.

THE UPJOHN COMPANY

■ ■ ■

NYSE Symbol: UPJ

In the past decade, pharmaceutical drugs have been one of the strongest sectors of our economy. Their outlook for the next decade is equally impressive because the United States spends over $500 billion a year on health care.

We think we have identified the cream of this industry by screening the list down to just two companies—Merck and Upjohn. These two probably have the industry's finest research and development capabilities, as well as stellar records in getting early FDA approval for important new drugs.

Upjohn is one of the largest manufacturers of prescription drugs in the United States, specializing in steroids, antibiotics and oral antidiabetes agents. The company also has an important position in agricultural products.

Featured drugs by Upjohn include Xanax and Halcion, effective antidepressants; Motrin and Nuprin, for arthritis; Orinase and Micronase, antidiabetics; and Deresyn, a new, fast-acting antidepressant.

Recently, Upjohn's Regaine has been given a lot of attention in the press. It is a prescription minoxidil hair-growth product. As usual among new drugs, dramatic reported results are being questioned. The product has been approved, however, in thirty-eight nations, but still awaits FDA approval in the United States. Upjohn also has representation in popular nonprescription drugs: Cheracol cough syrup, Unicap vitamins and Kaopectate for diarrhea.

The foregoing products are well accepted and generate high profit margins, especially the prescription drugs. Still in the laboratory stage are three or four new formulations that are expected to significantly expand profits within the next three years.

Agricultural sector products include Tolvid, a vaccine for hogs. Upjohn also owns the Asgrow Seed Company, which produces such superior-quality cereals as oats, beans, corn and soybeans. The company also produces poultry breeding stock.

Upjohn is a well-sponsored name in Wall Street, with 188 million shares outstanding. Dividends are not high but they are durable, continuous since 1909 and increased in nine out of the past ten years.

One does not buy Upjohn for current yield, but its cumulative annual return should keep it well ahead of the Dow Jones Industrial Average for years to come. This meets our definition of a Fortress Stock: a sound investment for today and an even more valuable asset for tomorrow.

WEYERHAEUSER
COMPANY

■ ■ ■

NYSE Symbol: WY

Weyerhaeuser is one of America's great natural resource companies. Headquartered in Tacoma, Washington, Weyerhaeuser owns over 6 million timberland acres in the United States, mostly on the West Coast, along with producing rights to over 12 million timber-bearing acres in Canada.

Based on this impressive standing inventory, the company has almost limitless capacity to supply the raw timber it requires for its diversity of wood products. It is a world leader in its field and an obvious Fortress selection.

Weyerhaeuser produces, in quantity, logs, board lumber, plywood, pulp, paperboard paper, newsprint and particle board—plus almost 20,000 square feet of shipping containers annually. Moreover, Weyerhaeuser generates about 60% of the energy it requires for its own operations. Forest products and paper account together for over 80% of annual sales.

Weyerhaeuser wood products enjoy board international sales, but logs (almost a billion cubic feet) are sold mainly to Japan, its largest export customer. Export sales have enjoyed a strong upturn as the dollar has declined.

The company has been a steady earner all along, but had demonstrated exceptional strength since 1985. Earnings per share almost quadrupled in the period 1985–1988 and should continue to rise. These earnings gains have made possible a 40% dividend increase in the last three years, along with a 3-for-2 stock dividend in 1988.

With its hefty treasury, Weyerhauser has been able to make significant acquisitions. In 1987, it purchased six corrugated container plants from Mead Corporation. In 1988, Weyerhaeuser announced construction of a new 1,200-ton-a-day kraft pulp plant at its Columbus, Mississippi, pulp and paper complex. This new facility will cost about $400 million.

With assets of $7 billion and annual sales on the same order, Weyerhaeuser is obviously a company of stature. It has a strong balance sheet, moderate debt, and, thanks to expansion and cost controls, it is steadily improving in profitability. Weyerhaeuser shares add diversity to our Fortress list and should deliver a series of dividend increases during the next year or two. Also noteworthy is the value of its wooded real estate, possibly attractive to a major acquisitor and especially valuable if inflation heats up. The only troublesome thing about Weyerhaeuser is the spelling of its name!

SUCCESSFUL PERSONAL INVESTING

This book was designed not as a text-book on investment theory but as a practical guide to successful personal investment. Fortified by this background information, you are now ready to proceed.

Get a good broker, preferably a member of the New York Stock Exchange, strongly financed and thoroughly dependable in the execution of orders and transfers and in the custody of securities. You will have little need for your broker's recommendations, since you have your own screened list and you do not aim to trade frequently or for quick speculative profits.

In general, plan your portfolio along the following lines: Fortress Stocks, 50% to 60%; bonds, 20% to 30%; money market funds (or CD's or short-term Treasuries),

10%; and gold, 10%. (I will discuss the merits of gold in a special section of this chapter.) Stick to this formula, bending it in favor of more bonds in later or retirement years, when the need became greater for higher dependable income.

The first order of business for building a portfolio is the beginning of a collection of the thirty Fortress Stocks as the portfolio's core. You do this by allocating funds out of income, or from a bonus, a lucky windfall or an inheritance. One of the best (and recommended) procedures is dollar-cost averaging. This is just a fancy way of saying that you allocate $1,000 (or units of $1,000) each year to the purchase of target stocks. That way, your $1,000 may buy only a few shares of a major stock in a year when it sells at 80, but a lot more in "down" years when the shares are quoted at 40. You can see that over the years you can build up a substantial holding at quite satisfactory prices. Nobody knows for sure what the market will do in any year, but in this way you are certain to buy cheap stock at some point and secure a reasonable average price.

Of course you will not buy all thirty Fortress Stocks at the outset, so pick ones you favor. For those of you who have present holdings, review them and weed out weak, overly speculative or slow-moving securities, replacing them with Fortress Stocks. If you stress dividend income, then you may want to start with Con Edison, Potomac Electric, Citicorp, Proctor & Gamble or NYNEX, which offer higher yields. If you prefer long-term growth, then consider first such companies as Upjohn, Merck or Minnesota Mining and Manufacturing. The thirty Fortress Stocks give you a wide and attractive selection.

A Word about Bonds
■ ■ ■

As to bonds, confine yourself to government (Treasuries), corporate (rated "A" or better), and quality municipals (if your tax bracket indicates their usefulness). I would also suggest a closed-end or mutual bond fund. This provides continuous supervision of your bond holdings, which is useful because bond issuers do not send out quarterly or annual statements. Thus, some bonds you hold might deteriorate seriously without your knowing about it. Bond funds also offer a wider diversification than you can provide, and the income from a substantial portfolio of bonds is consolidated into fewer monthly or quarterly interest distribution checks. That makes the accounting easier.

If you seek foreign bonds for exceptional yield, or want to own convertibles, a respected fund will supply the continuing analysis, judgment and decision-making skills you may lack.

As your portfolio grows and you enter or approach retirement years, you may want to improve your income with more bonds (up to 30% or so) and reduce Fortress holdings somewhat.

When the time comes to expand your bond holding, take careful note of the trend in interest rates. The variations on returns in this century, even on government bonds, have been amazing. In 1950, long-term Treasuries yielded 3%; in 1981, 15%. So watch carefully your entry into the bond market, and favor long-term Treasuries. As a general rule, thirty-year Treasury bonds are an excellent buy when they yield six full percentage points above the prevailing yield on the Dow Jones Stock. As a rule of thumb, buy long-term Treasuries when they yield 9% to 10% or higher.

The 10% of portfolio placed in money market or other short-term securities is useful. Everybody should have some assets in a money market fund to assure early availability of capital without risk or loss of principal and to have money at hand in an emergency.

Gold: Man's Most Cherished Portable Asset
■ ■ ■

There is a lot of nonsense being written about gold by economists and analysts who display their misinformation about its history and importance in the world economy.

The renowned economist Keynes called gold a "barbarous relic." He was wrong. For over six thousand years, gold has been man's most cherished portable asset, and it still is. For over three thousand years, gold served as the predominant monetary metal in commerce and trade. As a long-term standard of value it has no equal. Portable, indestructible, malleable and lustrous, it was valued first as an ornament in jewelry and utensils. It became, later on, an indispensable form of money, having been minted in coins of uniform size and weight as far back as 560 B.C.

GOLD-BACKED MONEY

For a century (1816–1914), the British pound sterling was the most acceptable unit of money throughout the world, and during that entire period it was convertible into gold at a fixed rate. From 1879 to 1933, the United States was on a gold standard, with paper dollars redeemable into gold at the rate of $20.67 an ounce. In mid-1933, it became illegal for Americans to own gold in bar, bullion, coin or gold certificate. Illegal possession was punishable by heavy fines. Convertibility of dollars was canceled.

In 1934 the United States had a gold-reserve standard dollar. It was backed by gold, valued at $35 an ounce, but Americans could not exchange their dollars for gold. Only central banks of foreign countries were permitted such exchange.

In 1971 President Richard Nixon closed "the gold window"—no more exchanges. The price of gold was set adrift, moving up to $48 an ounce in the free market within a year. But the United States kept most of its gold in Fort Knox and today owns 241 million ounces, valued on the books at $42.20 an ounce. France's store of gold is valued "at the market." Most leading nations own huge supplies of gold, and over 35% of all gold in use is owned by central banks as monetary reserves of last resort.

Today, however, no currency is backed by gold, and the national monetary units—the franc, pound, mark, yen and dollar—all trade with great price volatility in a kaleidoscopic relationship with one another. Neither the dollar nor any other currency provides the stable purchasing power of currencies previously backed by gold. Many economists, indeed, have suggested a return to some form of gold standard.

Gold remains important, traded twenty-four hours a day around the world, and is still sought as a reliable store of stable purchasing power in the event of the return of inflation. There will always be buyers for gold.

NO GLUT IN GOLD

There is frequent comment in the financial press that gold is becoming a "glut" metal, by virtue of all the new mines coming into production. There is no glut. It is true that when gold hit $850 an ounce on January 20, 1980, the profit potential caused hundreds of gold-mining companies to be formed. Gold mining is profitable. The average producer in North America can surface the metal for $250 an ounce or less, and most

African mines produce gold at below $200 an ounce. Even with all the newer mines entering and expanding their production—Newmont, Echo Bay, Freeport McMoran, Galactic, Glamis and others—the world production of gold has increased only about 4% a year since 1981. Annual world gold production in 1987 was about 1,350 tons for the Western-bloc world and 325 tons from Communist countries.

The world supply of gold—the above-ground store—is now about 100,000 metric tons: only enough to fill the lower half of the Washington monument. This represents about 90% of all the gold that was ever mined, a tribute to the durability of the metal. Of that amount, about 20% is available for trading or purchase among the commodity markets, institutions, inventories of jewelers or industrial gold suppliers, gold dealers and investors. Over 35% of this 100,000 tons is locked up in the vaults of central banks. Gold is, and has ever remained, a scarce metal.

World mining production per year is around 1,650 tons, and increasing, due to new mines opening. Production has also been stimulated by a low-cost leaching process that makes open-pit mining of low-grade ores profitable.

Now for the demand side. How does annual visible demand compare with the production of new gold? We have some fairly reliable figures for the western world. According to a recent report, the total gold consumption in the non-Communist countries was as follows:

Usage	Metric Tons
Jewelry	828
Coins	327
Dentistry	51
Electronics	123
Other Use	56
TOTAL DEMAND	1,385 tons

The jewelry demand is price sensitive. When gold was cheap (around $40 an ounce), in 1970, jewelry consumption reached an all-time high of 1,062 tons. It dipped by 40% in 1980 when gold peaked at $850 an ounce.

Coins and medallions are on the increase all over the world. The leading bullion coins (lacking a numismatic value) are the American Eagle, the Canadian Maple Leaf, the Chinese Panda and the South African Krugerrand. (The Krugerrand has been discontinued due to the U.S. boycott, but 50 million coins were sold up to 1985.) All of these coins are basically one ounce of gold, though smaller units of one-half, one-quarter and one-tenth of an ounce are also available. Coins are sold by dealers at a premium of 3% to 8% over the daily quote for gold.

Industrial uses of gold are rising, especially in electronics, in goldplate consumer goods and in protective and detective devices. Gold is an excellent conductor of electricity and is used in insulation of buildings and as a protective coating on space rockets.

The difference between the non-Communist world's freshly mined supply (1,350 tons) and total demand is supplied by recycled gold, imports (mainly from India) and unloading by investors.

On the demand side, the principal variable is the purchase by investors and hoarders and by central banks. When the market crashed on October 19, 1987, thousands of investors bought gold as a refuge from insecurity in the stock market. This demand might well have sent up the gold price, except for the fact that, in November, the Soviet Union sold gold heavily to pay for its grain imports.

Expectations for a rising price are based on: (1) steadily rising investor and hoarder demand for bullion and coins, (2) advice of financial planners to place 5% to 10% of investor portfolios in gold, and (3) fear of inflation.

Those who buy bullion coins—the American Eagle, Canadian Maple Leaf and Chinese Panda, for example—should do well. Collector coins—the U.S. Double Eagles, French Napoleon and Austrian Corona—should also gain.

There are some excellent gold stocks to investigate: Placer Dome, Newmont Gold and Homestake Mining, all on the New York Stock Exchange; Echo Bay Mining on the American Exchange; and Agnico-Eagle on the Toronto Exchange. These are all well-managed producers with long life ore bodies.

You should have some gold (up to 10%). Don't risk your capital by speculating in gold on the Commodity Exchange. If you stick to coins and the stocks suggested you will come out way ahead in four years. There have always been buyers of gold as a hedge against inflation and as a shelter from wars, riots and the like.

A Final Word on Stock Investing
■ ■ ■

Our major tenet is patient, long-term holding of high-grade common stocks of stature. It may take a while to own all thirty Fortress Stocks, but shop from this list and watch for price dips that may make one or two especially attractive.

Adhering to a planned program will keep you from tragic error. Use the Fortress list as your target for expansion. The usefulness of a portfolio design like the above is demonstrated by the October 1987 crash, when the blue chips held the line far better than lesser securities, in particular over-the-counter stocks that plunged drastically. The crash also proved again the folly of buying on margin and reemphasized the need to keep some portion aside in money market funds.

Over the years you may be tempted many times by an aggressive broker who phones you, urging a "hot" speculation, good for a swift and profitable turn. Plan to say *No!* Nobody knows the short-term trends in the market. October 19, 1987, proved that, and don't fall for a "pitch" to buy options or index futures for fast, leveraged profits. Seventy percent of all options wind up a total loss. The broker will be the one buying the Mercedes, not you!

If you follow an orderly program it can serve for years. Build your own citadel of income and gain around Fortress Stocks. And sleep well!

A Time to Sell
■ ■ ■

Don't sell on rumor, hearsay or the frantic urging of some eager-beaver broker. Never mind if others you know pursue a different style. The program of patient retention of classic stocks has built fortunes for thousands, and it can do the same for you.

Don't confuse speculation with investment. Speculation is essentially a series of short swings. Most speculators expect to make their "score" within months. Speculators are an "itchy" lot.

Conversely, no common stock is a "forever" holding, and many events may occur in a company's life that indicate its stock should no longer be held. Such things as a drastic decline in earnings, loss of markets due to obsolescence or competition, expansion or acquisition, or just plain poor management may move great corporations downhill. Look at the dismal descent in International Harvester, Johns Manville, Public Service of New Hampshire, and Amax emerging from gross over-investment in molybdenum.

There are certainly times when stocks should be sold on fundamental grounds, and no portfolio, even our Fortress list, is immune. All portfolios demand regular surveillance. But do not trade good stocks in and out. Buy the Fortress issues and hold them for the companies' higher earnings, dividends and price of their common stock over the years, but still keep an eye on them at regular intervals.

Plan to keep informed by reading the daily financial pages and perhaps *The Wall Street Journal* and Forbes magazine. Watch for and read carefully the quarterly and annual reports you receive. Note particularly mergers or acquisitions or development of a new product (positive signs), or any sharp changes in earnings or drastic change in management (which can be either positive or negative signs).

In addition to sharp variations in the affairs of corporations, which may suggest prompt purchase or sale of their shares, the condition of the market as a whole deserves attention. No one should buy at the top of a bull market or sell in panic near the bottom of a bear market. But how do you tell what stage the market is in right now? This is important to every financial institution and to 47 million individual share-owners.

What are some of the historic benchmarks or guidelines? The flow of the Dow Jones average gives us some clues. First, there is the historic Dow high of 2,722 established August 12, 1987, and low of 41.2 in July 1932. That's the range.

Within that, stock prices became dangerously high when the dividend yields of the Dow stocks averaged below 3%; they became attractive for purchase when they yielded 6%. The market has proved too high when

Dow shares sold at twenty-four times earnings and low and desirable when shares sold at six times earnings.

When stocks sell at 2½ times book value they are overpriced, but they become desirable at below book value. (Book value is the ratio between a company's assets and its liabilities.)

Accordingly, the Dow Jones price charts, which illustrated all the foregoing changes, are constantly referred to, and document where we are in perspective, whether in a bull or bear market.

All of us can benefit if we buy when the market climate is right, and when we get early notice of substantial downspins. Most of us are never completely out of the market, however. Early liquidation of stocks before they turn sour is important for maximizing one's gains. If a stock you own is consistently increasing in sales and profits at a rate of 20% or better annually, however, it is seldom wise to sell, even though the general market is moving off. Stand firm. Many people lose money by "itchy" sales of good stocks when rational retention would have made them rich. How many people are crying today because they sold IBM, Coca-Cola, Squibb, Exxon and the like some years back. "Whoever looks back in the stock market dies of remorse!"

With our thirty Fortress Stocks, we have selected a group of choice securities that solves most of the problems investors have and structures a program for success and contentment. This program should keep you from straying into many of the less-proven products and investment packages promulgated by brokerage houses, designed more to build commission profits for the firm than a balanced portfolio for clients.

Happiness is not only a stock that lets you sleep at night, but an elite collection of such stocks—our own thirty Fortress Stocks.